Published by Crooked Wall Press
Copyright © 2020 Jarod K. Anderson
All rights reserved
ISBN: 9798572931358

Thank you to the Smithsonian for the use of our cover image, "Study of Thistle Plants" by Sophia L. Crownfield (1862–1929)

# Field Guide to the Haunted Forest

Jarod K. Anderson

# Author's Note:

Poetry is an odd creature. Some of the work in this collection feels like poetry to me, the poetry I grew up writing and studying. Some of it feels more like a cousin to poetry. Yet, I believe all the text in this collection belongs here. This book focuses on the ideas and themes that matter to me. Gratitude to nature. Magic hiding in plain sight. The beauty of impermanence and our close kinship with the world we inhabit. Many of these poems started as social media posts or fragments of scripts for The CryptoNaturalist, my fiction podcast about strange nature and a man who finds beauty and meaning in the unusual. I hope the ideas in this book are useful to you. They have been very useful to me.

Jarod K. Anderson
Delaware, Ohio
November, 2020

Thank you to Leslie J. Anderson, a wonderful poet, editor, and partner.

Thank you to my parents, Molly and Dave Anderson for their endless enthusiasm and encouragement.

Thank you to Mark Travis for helping me untangle my thoughts and return to regular writing.

# Technically Speaking

You can look at any human life
as the sum of a complex collection of chemical reactions,

in much the same way as you can look at any beautiful painting
as a simple collection of pigments,

Which is to say,
you can miss the point of anything.

# Lump

A lump of iron formed in the heart of a red super-giant.
So long ago.
So far from here.
There was a silent explosion.
There was a trip across lightyears, cold and hard,
drifting like a dandelion seed through a dark forever.
The lump came to Earth.
It was forged into a sword.
A hammer.
A ring.
It flowed red through the blood of a leaping deer,
but it was still the star. The long, dark journey.
Crimson in the veins of a sleeping child,
but still the silent explosion.
And it brought what it was
wherever it traveled.

# Sit With Me

I'm not trying to write a tailored suit.
I'm trying to write boot socks, warm from the dryer.
There's an endless autumn in me,
scenting my thoughts like campfire smoke.
I write for the weather I know.

# Woodland You

It's easy to look at the contours of a forest and feel
a bone deep love for nature.
It's less easy to remember that the contours of your own body
represent the exact same nature.
The pathways of your mind.
Your dreams,
dark and strange as sprouts curling beneath a flat rock.
Your regret,
bitter as the citrus rot of old cut grass.
It's the same as the nature you make time to love.
That you practice loving.
The forest. The meadow. The sweeping arm of a galaxy.
You are as natural as any postcard landscape
and deserve the same love.

# Home Safety Tip

If you are awoken by a strange sound,
make a stranger sound.

If there's no response,
congratulations.

You are the monster now.

Get out of bed.
You don't need to sleep anymore.

Now, all you need are the shadows
and the endless whispers of dark corners.

# Naming the River

The water in your body is just visiting.
It was a thunderstorm a week ago.
It will be an ocean soon enough.
Most of your cells come and go like morning dew.
We are more weather pattern than stone monument.
Sunlight on mist. Summer lightning.
Your choices outweigh your substance.

# The Chain

You were once very much part of your mother's body.

The same is true for your mother and her mother
and so on back to the beginning.
It's a biological chain that stretches back to the first living cell
awakening in a young ocean
millions of years before the first spoken name.

We are links in that chain.
Can you feel its weight?
A clear path back to ancient waters.

You are here. In modernity. As familiar as thirst.
Just remember what else you are.
Your mother. Her mother. The ancient seas beneath a thin, new sky.

# Host

To invading germs, you are a jungle
full of hungry tigers.

To your gut bacteria, you are a warm orchard
of perpetual bounty.

To your eyelash mites, you are a walking fortress
and a mountaintop pasture.

How many generations have you hosted?
What do they name the wilderness of you?

# The Wood

When you were born, your enthusiasm was a red flame atop a mountain of fuel. As you age, the fuel burns low. No one warns you. Yet, with intention, you can learn to feed that warming fire long after the fuel you were born with is ash on the wind. Be kind to yourself. Learn this.

They say cut all the wood you think you will need for the night, then double it. Cut it during the daylight when fuel seems irrelevant. Dead limbs hanging low, sun-dried, hungry for fire. The night can be longer than we expect. The wind can be colder than we predict. The dark beneath the trees is absolute. Gather the fuel. Double it.

# Family Resemblance

Our blood is red because of the iron we inherited from the Earth.
Iron to bind the oxygen from trees and phytoplankton.
Our blood and breath are hand-me-downs.
The landscape is not scenery.
It's family. Notice the resemblance.

Our blood is mostly water.
Iron to bind oxygen, built using the energy of sunlight.
Water. Earth. Air. Fire.
You may feel separated from the natural world,
but just look at what you are.
Look at how you live.
You are not born to this place. You are born of this place.

Take one square meter of your bedroom,
of the deepest abyss of sunless sea,
of the brutal emptiness of interstellar space.
Put them side by side and see the harmony.
They are all children of the same natural laws.

Our bodies speak of contradiction.
Bones and soft tissue. Teeth and lips. Sensitive resilience.
What strong family resemblance we share
with the landscapes that shaped us.
Wind and stone. Rivers and oaks.
This old dance of opposing forces
creating a unified whole.

# Unscripted

We all consume so many purposefully crafted stories
that it's easy to forget life doesn't follow
conventional narrative structure.
We can't wait for our climax.
We don't have character arcs.
We live and then we don't.
There is no culmination in success or failure.
We are not curated collections of achievements or mishaps.
Don't fear you won't be good enough.
Just be here.
Present in this dance between joy and sorrow.
The plot is happening now.
Today is the story of you and me.

# The Treatment

I can't say spending time in nature heals depression.
For me, the outdoors changes sadness from a pain
to be endured to a state to be experience.
It's still sadness.
But in the context of green growing things
under a limitless sky, sadness is simplified.
Not a wound. A tile in the mosaic.

Even so, depression needs more.

I resisted trying therapy for a long time
because I thought I was too smart for it.
Here's the thing.
You can't think your way out of depression
any more than you can think your way out of drowning.
Asking for a life-jacket is more important
than knowing the physics of buoyancy.

# The Text

You are a unique sentence built from the alphabet of our universe.
The letters were here before you and the story will march on
long after you've been read,
but you will forever be a part of the definitive text of existence.
It's too late for you not to matter.

# Plain as Day

Your eye is a collection of cells
that evolved to borrow radiation
from a fiery ball of superheated hydrogen and helium
in order to gather information
about objects outside your physical reach.

Vision is a kind of divination
shaped and fueled by a cosmic inferno.
This can't be true.

It very much is.

# Identity

There's a silver bell in your rib cage.
When you're trying to fall asleep, you feel for it,
like a tongue mapping a chipped tooth.

One day,
you'll find it and it will ring cold and clear as an autumn lake.
That sound will be who you are,
warm certainty like a belly full of hot soup,
until it fades.

Then, you'll search again.

# Sentry

Kindness. Gentleness. Empathy.

These things are fires shining in the forest night.
They must be tended,
but in tending them we are illuminated.

We become a target for things that thrive in darkness.

So, as ever, love is risk.
And, as ever,
worth the danger.

# The Whole

All living things are the same living thing,
a branching tree spreading from a shared past.

This unified creature grows in four dimensions,
and the illusion of separation we see here
on the budding branch-tips
appears because we can't view time
the way we see our own vital hands.

It's as real as the moment mitochondria moved in to stay.
And maybe, in the end, we'll feel it like warm coffee on the tongue,
like skin against skin.

I wish I could wander back through my ancestors
like a steppingstone path.

To Ireland. To Africa.
Past organisms that were never named by humans.
To the sunlit waters where life began to feel its own strange power.
To the forest of hands that lifted me up into my own simple life.

I wish I could know the whole,
so I could love it more completely.

# Candle Facts #1

If you whisper a secret to a candle flame,
then all fire everywhere will know that secret.

The words will crackle in every campfire
and churn like an ocean deep in the belly of the Earth.

Fire will translate your words to smoke and ash,
telling no one but the sky.

# Together in Absurdity

The entirety of your personality resides in an organ the size of a guinea pig encased in the living stone of your skull.

Your thoughts are spun like cotton candy from flesh and electricity and you expect to be perfect?

All the billions of humans on Earth are living
this same strange, awkward truth.
There's a reason we have empathy.
We need it.

# The Big Bang

The universe is an ongoing explosion.

That's where you live.

In an explosion.

Of course, we absolutely don't know what living is.
We don't know what happens in the gulf
between molecules and cells.

Sometimes, atoms arranged in a certain way just get very, very haunt-
ed.

That's us.

When an explosion explodes hard enough,
dust wakes up and thinks about itself.

And then writes about it.

# Many Hands

The world will always be troubled.
This is true.

You deserve to feel happy and comfortable.
This is also true.

If you feel the first truth undermines the second, I offer this:

Own a share of the virtuous work toward solutions.
Don't burden your worth with global outcomes.

The good and the evil are happening concurrently.
The choice to focus on the good is itself
a way to defy the evil.

# Reaction

The first living cell on Earth was a spark.
It ignited a chain reaction that thundered across millions of years,
an evolving blaze of lives and needs and firsts and lasts.

The whole of that raging fire of history and happenstance
burns inside you right now.
You are that continuity of matter and motion.

Your irrational fear of centipedes.
An old scar like a barbed hook.
The effortless bravery of your kindness.

You are the flame racing down the fuse.

# Thoughts Like Ivy

Your brain,
the seat of your consciousness,
is as natural as a leaf.

It arose in the world in the same way as a finch's wing.
A cricket's song.

Wherever you are right now,
the part of you that's awake and reading this
is in nature.

There's a temptation to think of ourselves as separate
here in the warm quarters of civilization.
But our thoughts?

Our thoughts echo from an ancient wilderness.

# Potential

You can be still while the world is whirling.
You can be silent while your heart is thundering.
You can be alone while your memory is teeming.

You can live forever in the span of a moment.
You can grow kindness in the soil of hatred.
You can decide purpose. You can decide victory.

# Vulnerable

You are not safe.
Your birth was reckless.
Lightning strikes without reason.
Countless simple mishaps may be fatal.
To live is to collect risk like a bee collects nectar.

Yet there is hope in fragility.

Our goal was never safety.
Our success is not measured in forever.
Our years are seasoning, but the meal is meaning.
Our task is to become our truest selves and to smile
at the knowledge that we will not succeed.

# Limits

You won't see most of this planet.
Under each rock.
Beneath the water.
Secrets of air and soil.

Can you feel the joy behind this limitation?
That there is always a new thing to discover,
a new way to grow,
is one of the sweetest parts of living,

and it's free and inexhaustible.

# Every Life is a Sound

The soft susurrus of jellyfish who have never known the shore.
The sharp sizzle of deer fleeing through autumn corn.

These sounds belong to the same unfinished poem as you
and your fistful of years like copper coins.

It wouldn't be poetry without you.

# The Impossible

Bats can hear shapes.
Plants can eat light.
Bees can dance maps.

We can hold all these ideas at once and feel
both heavy and weightless
with the absurd beauty of it all.

# Unwritten

50,000 years ago,
an elk was struck by lightening and lived.

The ache of it stayed in her bones the rest of her life.
There was no human there to see it or record it in words,

yet it's just as much a part of earth's essential history as any song
lingering in a billion human minds.

# Calibration

Weigh a leaf in your palm.
Imperceptible.
A green whisper.
A cool nothing.
Weigh it again in your lungs,
with the iron in your blood.
Feel your genes clinging to those soft green cells like ivy on an oak.
Weigh the leaf once more with your love.
Trust this measure most.

# Blueprint

If you write out the basic facts of trees,
but framed as technology,
it sounds like impossible sci-fi nonsense.

Self-replicating, solar-powered machines
that synthesize carbon dioxide and rainwater
into oxygen and sturdy building materials
on a planetary scale.

What do we make that compares?

# Fossil

The fossil is not the animal.

The fossil is not the bones of the animal.

The fossil is the stone's memory of the bones of the animal.

And that's a poetry older than words.

# Candle Facts #2

A lit candle is a tiny, flickering animal
standing on top of all the food it will eat in its lifetime.

A candle is a leash.

They let us tame an ancient, devouring force of nature,
older than life,
and stick it in a little jar on the shelf.

A candle is a pet god.

# Thanks to Birds

Birds are dinosaurs who shrugged off a couple apocalypses.
Some eat bone marrow.
Some drink nectar.
They outswim fish in the sea.
They smile politely at gravity's demands.
I am grateful to see them. I am grateful to feed them.
I am grateful to know them.

# Losing

Our muscles are prompted to grow by failure,
healing from countless micro-injuries.

Our minds, science, and technology
are similarly nourished by defeat.

We are creatures born to thrive
on the borderlands of ruin.

Home is a valley between saw-toothed peaks of loss.
Here we sow failure and harvest miracles.

## Seriously Though

If you can make peace with the unlikely fact
that squids the size of school buses patrol the dark oceans
at a depth that would crush you to paste,

then I have faith you can also make peace with the unlikely fact
that you are worthy of all the happiness you have imagined.

# Orcas

Somewhere, there are orcas.

I'm in my little gray house in Ohio
surrounded by the stale air of winter indoors,

but somewhere there are orcas.

It's an easy fact to forget.
It's easy to shrink your world to what you can see.

But thankfully, somewhere, there are orcas.

Sometimes, my world is all sun-faded plastic
scrawled along the roadside in a scribble of petty meanness,

but somewhere there are orcas.

We all know facts that are as inert as chalk dust,
but some knowledge is medicine.

# Flawless

Things that are perfect
are dead things.

Empty things.

A silence beyond change or challenge.
An endpoint.
A blank page.

You are a wonderfully messy thing.

An impossible thing made of salt
and rainwater.
Meat and electricity.

A dream with teeth.

You're too good for perfection.

# Crush

Today you did things that humans 50 years ago wouldn't believe
and 200 years ago would struggle to imagine.

You know the names of planets
and the shapes of the bones inside you.

You comprehend death and make art.
You are a surpassingly strange animal, worthy of study.

I love you.

# The Truth About Owls

You flinch at leaf shadows
tumbling across your driveway
and the shadows notice you flinching.

The thought gets under their skin,
starts them asking questions to your back
as you walk away.

"Are we something to fear?"

Two nights later,
the shadows pile into three dimensions,
hop twice, and fly off on soundless wings.

# Economics

We borrow our atoms.
The universe owns them.

The universe borrows our love and wonder.
Those belong to us.

# Nameless

Remember this:
Someone made-up the word "sky."

Likewise the word "wolf."
The words "leaf" and "raindrop."

Words are jewels.

Precious to us, but small and finite.

Forget these words and try to name these things anew.
You will feel their scope and meaning weigh upon your mind.

Pour a new word into the sky and see it fade like smoke.

Look for the noise that equals the reality of wolves.

How will you wrap such things up in syllables
And set them upon your tongue.

# Soft

Our fingers are built more for feeling than fighting.
Nerve endings prioritized over talons or claws.

Our relatively modest strength.
Our long, vulnerable road to adulthood.

Our species' success is the story of betting
on understanding over brutality.

It's the wise, patient bet.

# Psst

The universe is an event, not a place.
Don't seek to own.
Witness.

# Entangled

The problem with history is that it's full of spiders.
They scribbled webs over the invention of doorways
and crawled into the bellies of our sleeping orators.

Show me the liar saint that never killed or cursed one.
And when we load the beds and dark corners into ships
like silver needles tugging our thin threads through space

we might declare a hasty victory over recluse and funnel-web.
But, they'll be there. Strung up just at face-level
in the dark paths between the rocks and suns.

# Pact

Iron in birds' inner ears
helps them navigate using the Earth's magnetic field.

In other words,
the birds carry within them a piece of the Earth,

a talisman, which speaks to the Earth and whispers
its knowledge back to the birds.

Hey.

Your matter recalls cosmic explosions
and you tasted oblivion before you learned your own name.

Fear nothing.

# Home

An ant crosses your carpet.
A spider weaves a pattern older than mammals beneath your stairs.

Just nod,
breathe,
and think,

good.
It's all still here.
The forest, the mountains, the desert.

At home in my home.

The sterile white box is the stranger.
Not the ant.
Not the spider.

# Truth and Fact

"Love is just chemicals."

Yeah?

So is the churning inferno of the sun.
So is the bedrock of the earth.
So is the living fountain of a blooming cherry tree.

If you need to call upon the word "magic"
to fully appreciate the beauty of all that which is vivid and real,

do so.

Truth and fact are sisters, not twins.

# Statecraft

Night is Earth's shadow.
Your shadow is a tiny, you-shaped night.

Your night and Earth's night know each other.

They have conversations that you can't hear and wouldn't understand
anyway.

Don't begrudge them this.

Your shadow is an embassy for the nation of you.
It's wise to foster diplomacy
with a neighbor older than starlight.

# Worthless

One dangerous illusion of modernity is the link
between cost and value.

Could we afford the true cost of rain?

Can we calculate a price for the work of phytoplankton
producing the oxygen we need?

Our survival will require us to understand value independent of cost.

# Relativity

There.
Now.
A sharp stone juts from an icy sea.
crowded with gulls screaming accusations at a flinty sky,

the wind hides daggers and beneath the waves
something rich in teeth swims lazy circles.

Here.
Now.
I hope this truth makes your current surroundings seem
more warm and welcoming.

# Owl

The best poems are owls.
A reflection of the landscape,
but singular and strange,

smooth and effortless as smoke.
A trick of the eye that scatters bones in the underbrush,
hard and real.

## This and More

The world is the sound of tree shapes
decoded in a bat's brain.
The world is electric fields
flexing in the mind of a shark.
The world is a landscape of scents,
recalled by a wolf like an old friend.
The world is a mosaic of temperature shifts
on the tip of a python's snout.
The world is you
making meaning
from marks on this page.

# Your Maker

The sun isn't alive.
It's better than alive.

It swims,
self-sustaining,
through endless void.

All we in its orbit think and do
is a byproduct
of its audacious existence.

# Waiting Up

Autumn is a kind of nightfall.
Plants and animals withdraw into sleep,
curling inward around the warm spark of their lives,

waiting for the spring dawn.

We who stay awake
are witnesses to the dormant, secret times.
Seasonally nocturnal.

We keep watch through the cold and dark.

# Ownership

Fish flashed in mountain streams long before the first human.
Honey was sweet and falling snow was graceful
before a person noticed such things.
This world is not here for us.
We are simply fortunate to live here.

# Almost Certainly a Time Traveler

I think my bones remember, even if I don't.
My teeth feel like time-traveler's teeth.
Temporality skitters along my femur
Like centipedes on a fallen branch.

I know how to do it.
When I concentrate on the idea,
Schematics bloom inside my skull,
Vivid diagrams pulsing with déjà vu.

It would take all I own and more,
An absolute and final turning away
From the people I love. From simple comforts.
A gamble aimed at erasing its own necessity.

I'm no daredevil with causality. No crusader.
Erasing the old atrocities would kill our present
And cowardly and selfish as I am
I wouldn't do it for lottery winnings.

I know I wouldn't because I haven't.

But I can imagine reasons
And I ache with the feeling that my life,
As familiar and yielding as an old paperback,
Means that the mission was accomplished.

I am desperately thankful for my own fingers
As if I gave reality a fat lip just to keep them
And each word my wife speaks, love or shopping lists,
Is worth innovation bordering on absurdity.

I can almost remember doing it.

On evenings after work, I take inventory of my life.
I do it for the version of me that made the leap
And if I was bold and brilliant and risked all,

Then, as I watch sitcom reruns in bed,
Safe and whole with my wife softly snoring,
I know I have been well rewarded for my efforts.
I owe it to myself to notice.

# Spoiler Alert

I just read ahead to the last page of your life and it turns out that you were always worthy of love and hope and surpassing kindness.

# Dying Practice

Every memory is a ghost and the house they haunt is you.

27-year-old me is gone from the world,
but echoes of him remain.

The same is true for 17-year-old me
and 7-year-old me.

Those people no longer exist.

But I hear their footsteps in the attic,

walking where I can't
where I will join them
in the memory of a future me.

# Solar Power

When the winds talked back,
there was an ember on the tongue of the world.
Each word glowed red as fresh-dug clay.

We didn't know the words,
so we pressed our ears to conch shells
and listened to the roar of our own veins.

Some blood rumbled shame
like the wordless chug of an engine
and others said, "all is well and always will be."

Our blood said to plant.

Seeds like sleek white birds
that smelled of ozone before a storm
and would spin on your open palm
forever.

They were not fast-growing crops
and the fields seemed fallow
under sunsets that rusted
trust and expectation,

but the day came.

At first, they looked like foxgloves
with fresh shoots spun from liquid glass
blooming chrome and circuitry.

They climbed hundreds of feet
and when they met the wind,
they greeted it in its own language,
syllables old as oceans.

The fruit we harvested
took our thirst and our hunger
and sizzled on our lips like rain on pavement.

When the winds talked back,
there was an ember on the tongue of the world
and we turned toward the heat like flowers toward the sun.

# Lifespan

A firefly lives two months.
There are bristlecone pines standing today that have lived 5,000 years.

The vital dignity of each of these species is not measured in time.
Both are perfection.

Treat your time likewise.
Your moments deserve the same careful attention as your years.

# In the End

You were a part of the sky on loan to a body.

A part of the sea that awoke to thought.

A part of the Earth who borrowed a name.

The essential piece of you that lingers is the love and knowledge that you set in motion while you moved through the waking world.

You are nature and nature will go on,

but there is kindness that only you can choose to bring to the world.

# Our Craft

People make meaning like bees make honey.

Gathering experiences and images,
synthesizing them into something new,
rich,
uniquely ours.

Respect the meaning you make,
the family you choose,
the wisdom you craft,

sweet and golden on your tongue.

# Mercy

The old you buzzes around your skull like a bee
in the kitchen window.
Don't swat it.
Be kind.

We must hope that our current selves will one day step aside to make
room for better versions of us.
Shuttle the old you outside in a mason jar.
Let it climb onto the lilac in the sun.

# A Time for Choice

You are the mountain, but awake.
You are the rain, but breathing.
You are the forest, but unanchored.
You are the soil, but with choice.
You are the sunlight, but dreaming.

Soon, you will be these things again. Mountain. Rain. Forest. Sunlight.

So, what will you do until then?

# Endpoint

One day,
your story will end
and all the choices you made will be frozen
like an insect in the amber of history.

Friend, this isn't meant to be grim.
Just a reminder that you are building something that will one day be
whole and complete.
So, build with purpose.

# Better to be Safe

When he thinks of it,
my father tries to talk over the rain
like his voice is a place of its own
where we won't see my mother
closing her eyes each time we pass
the great grey smudge of a semi.

When we have a quiet moment,
in the safe places, she says the trucks
make her think of tasting her own blood,
like a penny on her tongue with one
cheek on the wet pavement
that should be cold, but isn't.

She tells me how the sky looks green
just before the tornado comes
and plucks the roof out into nothing
like the way black ice makes the breaks
useless, makes the steering wheel useless
makes joints, tendons, muscles useless.

When they found her cancer,
she shaved her own head, standing
at the kitchen counter while my father
canceled their cruise ship reservations.
She waited for weeks to tell my brother
and me. She said I was too busy
for an extra worry.

# Unlearning Death

When we die, they may bury us or collect our ashes, but remember this: from baby teeth to skin cells and everything in between, most of the matter that has worn your name is already spread throughout the world. We bury our remains in the soil of our lifetimes.

Can you feel it? So many of the cells that have formed the community of your body have returned to nature. Most of the water that has fueled your life has returned to the sea. The substance of your form is not fixed. It flows like a river to and from the wilderness.

Moss doesn't think about being alive and mountains don't consider themselves to be dead. Death has no place in the vocabulary of nature. To worry about death is to forget that we, the moss, and the mountains are all part of an undiminished whole that isn't measured in breaths.

# Holy

Let nature be your church.

Let the trees be your temple.

Let each nourishing breath be your sacred vow.

Let the shared spark of life be your holy order and,
if there is one prayer you can whisper into the ear of the world,

let it be "thank you."

## About the Author:

Jarod K. Anderson lives in a white house between a forest and a graveyard. He writes and narrates The CryptoNaturalist podcast, a scripted, bi-weekly audio drama about a folksy narrator exploring bizarre places and impossible wildlife. You can find more of Jarod's writing in places like Asimov's, Escape Pod, and Apex Magazine.

Author Website:
www.jarodkanderson.com

The CryptoNaturalist: Available anywhere you find podcasts or stream directly from our website.
www.cryptonaturalist.com

Twitter: @CryptoNature
Facebook: /CryptoNaturalist
Instagram: @CryptoNaturalist

To support Jarod's work and gain access to exclusive content, visit Patreon.com/CryptoNaturalist

Publishing Note:

"Solar Power" originally appeared as "Planters' Season" in Star*Line, Fall 2016

"Almost Certainly a Time Traveler" originally appeared in Asimov's, March/April 2017

Made in the USA
Las Vegas, NV
16 December 2022

62865700R00046